WAKE UP TO YOUR WORTH

36 Life-Changing Lessons to guide you from Breakdown to Breakthrough

Claire Hearn

Illustrated by Sarah Watt

ISBN-13: 9798648887916

Cover design by: Sarah Watt
Photography by: Claire Hearn

CONTENTS

INTRODUCTION

I wrote this book as I was healing from the completion of a beautiful romantic relationship with a man who I lovingly refer to as my 'Earth Angel'. As the relationship wound down it exposed within me a lot of unhealed wounds and disempowering patterns of behaviour from my past that simply no longer served me. Having invested heavily into this connection I spent months feeling lost and unsure for myself, to the point where I reached my rock bottom over Christmas of 2019. Having lost my zest for life, I ended up in hospital.

Right then I had a choice – I could either continue on this path of self-sabotage and pity or I could climb out from underneath the rocks and reach once again for the sky. Thankfully I found the strength within me to choose the latter. Turning to the self-help gurus who I had followed for months on Instagram and YouTube coupled with filling my mind with inspiring books and the love of my family and friends – I started to empower myself once again. It was from this place that the idea for this book was born.

I've lived a pretty full life for my 36 years. I'm a woman who used to Police the streets of London, before becoming an Entrepreneur and then one day I changed my life all over again by relocating to Italy - a country where I didn't initially know anyone but where I felt a deep inner connection and belonging. Along the way I experienced mind blowing highs and numbing lows but all the while I was growing and changing into the woman I realise now, that I was always destined to be. I've had my fair share of heartache, perceived 'failures', successes and regret. I've been courageous, bold and brave. I've learnt a hell of a lot - both about myself and about this journey of life. The one common thread throughout all of my life experiences is that I have always loved helping and being of service to others, which is why writing this book felt the next natural step to take.

*Wake Up to Your Worth i*s a book designed to take your hand and guide you from those rock bottom moments in life that we all experience to having the awakening and breakthrough, that's always waiting for us on the other side. It's the exact Lessons I learnt - one for each of my 36 years - that helped to move me from my moment of Breakdown through to my very own Breakthrough. We quite often close off from our friends and family – and retreat within – when life gets tough. My desire for this book is that it can provide a source of comfort to help you in those moments, in rediscovering your worth.

You can choose to read this book cover to cover or as I love – treat it as a daily message from the Universe – and open it onto the page that you are called to. Whatever you decide, I want you to know that this book is there for you. It's there to enrich you, to nourish you and to open your eyes to your own personal situation, helping you to move forward in a strong, healthy way and not become a victim of your circumstances.

It's easy to say that life happens to us but everything, even the most painful situations – are always happening for our highest good. Know this, believe this and trust this.

This isn't some abstract self-help book – these are words from a woman who has been there, done that and ultimately come through it all the other side - a better, stronger version of myself. That is exactly what I wish for you.

I and this book are with you, every step of the way.

Love from Claire x
Instagram @lovefromclaire
www.lovefromclaire.com

"You've seen my descent; now watch my rising."

RUMI

1. KNOW YOUR WORTH

"Why do you keep putting yourself in situations that hurt you?"

Someone once said this to me – and as much as those words stung at the time – I realise looking back that there was absolute truth in them.

How many times have you stayed in a relationship with someone who disrespected you or kept hanging out with flaky friends? It's the ultimate act of self-sabotage to put up with or allow situations that leave you feeling unworthy. So why do so many of us do it?

The answer is very often the same. We accept the breadcrumbs and the less than ideal behaviours because we don't love ourselves enough to want better. At a deep, often sub-conscious level, we don't consider ourselves to be worthy enough to be treated right.

Let me tell it to you straight. You are worthy and you

are deserving of the very best that life has to give. Irrespective of your bank balance, skin colour, gender, sexuality or age - **You are 100% worthy.** It's time we stop giving our power away to others and actually begin to invest it back into ourselves and into our own self-worth.

This is where self-worth goes hand in hand with self-love. If you love yourself enough you won't allow yourself to be treated badly, you won't put up with situations that no longer serve you and you will create healthy boundaries that respect your worth. In a nutshell you will make yourself and how you feel, a number one priority.

When the relationship broke down that prompted this book, I realised just how unworthy I felt. I had given my all to something that wasn't deep down as reciprocated as I had believed. Rather than seeing it for what it was – a reflection of the other person and their own things they needed to work on – I took it to mean that there was something wrong with me. Perhaps it was the way I looked, my body, cultural differences, the fact I didn't cook a lot that was the problem.... I mean, SERIOUSLY.

The blunt truth was that I had disempowered myself massively. I had placed my self-worth in the hands of another. A pattern of behaviour which I later came to realise, had been evident in all of the romantic relationships I had had.

In this instance I wasn't loving myself enough to walk

away. Instead I was stubbornly wanting to try again, to keep putting up with the sub-standard behaviour, to keep being rejected.

There is a part of me that wishes that I could rewind a couple of months and shake some sense into me but as I know now it's all about appreciating the journey that has got me here and the personal growth that came with that. If this hadn't have happened, chances are that you wouldn't be reading this book, so actually there's a lot to be thankful for!

There's a number of ways we can start to love ourselves more and realise our worth. It all begins with your beliefs – the very heart of who you are as a person and what you think is possible for your life. Emotional Freedom Technique (otherwise known as Tapping) is an incredible free, painless technique that you can use to help with this. Tapping helps to shift the limiting blocks and beliefs you have within you, so that you can replace them with more empowering ones. *You can read more about this in Life Lesson 8 - The Life Changing Magic of Tapping.*

Other ways to love yourself more and know your worth include simple actions such as throwing away worn out clothes and discarding items that remind you of a shit time in your life – everything holds energy.

Take the time to evaluate friendships and relationships – are they serving you? Are they making you feel good? If not, is there anything that can be done to make things better? Or is it time to make new connections and meet new people, who are more in alignment with where you want to be?

Be real and honest with yourself in all areas of your life. The only way change is ever effected is if we go deep into ourselves and make those decisions and adjustments that quite often feel extremely uncomfortable, in the moment.

Knowing your worth and loving yourself are the catalysts for living your very best life. Gone are the days where you seek from others what you can give to yourself. It's like asking a monk for whisky. It's never going to happen. You can't get something from somebody who hasn't got what you want in the first place. It begins and ends with you. When you make the changes and value yourself more, your life will shift for the better. That is what it's all about.

Self-Worth Checklist

Here are some reminders of what having self-worth looks like. Find ways to make these an everyday part of your life;

- Respecting yourself and how you feel
- Creating healthy boundaries
- Walking away from what no longer serves you
- Appreciating just how incredible you are
- Only saying 'Yes' to what truly lights you up
- Following your desires and dreams
- Staying true to you at all times

2. KINDNESS IS ALWAYS REWARDED

I n Italy it's common to find people standing outside supermarkets asking for money. Sometimes
they will offer to help you in some way or other
times they simply open their hand. Either way I used
to be super sceptical. I used to think that I worked hard
for my money and resented giving it away for no appar-
ent good reason. All of that changed one day when my
eyes were finally opened up to the power of kindness.

It was a hot Summer afternoon and I was out shopping
with my 'Earth Angel'. He was looking at some retro
style sunglasses at one of the news-stands and although
he didn't buy any right then, he expressed an interest in
getting a new pair soon. Shortly afterwards we went to
the supermarket. As we walked through the exit there
was a man standing there holding an upturned cloth
cap, asking for money. I was my usual cynical self but
my 'Earth Angel' reached into his pocket and pulled

out the last of the coins he had on him and gave them to the man.

I remember questioning him endlessly as we walked back to his car, as to why he had done that and all he would say is "Good Karma".

As we approached his car, I noticed something on the floor near to his door. I took a closer look and couldn't believe what I saw – it was only a pair of retro style sunglasses! With it not being obvious where they had come from or who they belonged to, my 'Earth Angel' picked them up and with a knowing nod said once again, "Good Karma".

To some this may be a crazy coincidence but to me that was a moment I'll never forget. Not only did my 'Earth Angel' get his sunglasses but the significance is that it came on the back of an act of kindness, which had no expectation.

The biggest lesson I learnt that day is that when we are kind to others and to ourselves, not expecting anything in return, we are always blessed in infinite ways from the Universe.

Kindness is so often underrated in our society but honestly, it's one of the most powerful acts we as humans can do. Being kind can take many forms – whether that's looking out for your neighbour, offering support to a friend, holding a door open for a stranger or even simply deciding to look at life and others with more compassion and less judgement. However you decide to do it, make it your mission in life to be kind. Always.

* * *

3. SCRIPT YOUR LIFE

B elieve this when I say it – we are the sole creators of our lives. If there is something in our life, that we aren't happy with, we have the complete power to change it. Don't buy into the disempowering beliefs that we are somehow fated with the life we lead and that it's our destiny. You always have an opportunity to write a new story for yourself, even if your current reality screams otherwise.

I first learnt about Scripting through the powerful Law of Attraction works of Abraham Hicks – channelled through Esther and the late, Gerry Hicks. There are hundreds of YouTube videos with their teachings – so if you haven't heard of them before then this is a great place to start.

Now Abe as I call it, may take a little getting used to but once you do it will change your outlook on life completely – and I don't say that lightly. In one of their books, *'Ask and it is Given'*, I read about a powerful manifesting technique called Scripting.

This technique requires you to write about the life that you desire in all its delicious detail, as if it has *already* happened. This simple action of writing your desires sets a clear intention to the Universe and by re-reading it every single day, feeling into the emotion of your words – you set the wheels of manifestation into form. Of bringing your deepest, innermost desires to life. I get it – it sounds too good to be true but just like anything in life - don't knock it until you try it.

The key to Scripting though is not to get caught up wondering *how* it is going to happen. Instead it's about allowing yourself to be caught up in the feelings of excitement that you would feel if this was *now* your life. This really plays into the Law of Attraction because the Universe responds to your vibrations – to your feelings – whether they are as a result of your current life or how you would like your life to be. Either way the Universe delivers to you, experiences that are a vibrational match.

By writing your Script as if it has already happened you are training your brain to believe this is your reality and as a result the Universe responds accordingly.

I used this exact technique to manifest a completely different life for myself in a brand-new country, with no clue how it was going to happen.

It was January 1st 2018 and I had decided that I wanted something different for my life. I was deeply unhappy and unsatisfied with how things were going for me, even if on the surface it may have looked like everything was fantastic. Things are not always as they seem which is why we make such a mistake when we compare our lives to others.

That day I sat by the crackling log fire in my cottage, took a journal with the incredible cover, *'The Dream is Real'* and started my first Script. I wrote about my new life in Italy, about the amazing new friendships I had, about the work I had that enabled me to meet new people and deepen my knowledge of the Italian culture and about the new loving, romantic relationship I was enjoying. At this point I didn't know anybody in Italy and I had absolutely no logical idea how this was all going to unfold. All I did know was as crazy as the words sounded, they felt real to me. I was in complete alignment.

In the weeks that followed I listened to my inspired thoughts and took little steps every day. I set up a cultural exchange with an Italian family where I taught English and got to stay in Italy for a month, I applied for jobs and met new people. By July 2018 I had manifested about 80% of what I had written. One month later, I left for my new life in Italy.

Even now as I re-read that Script I wrote, in all its faded glory, I realise how even more of it is now my reality. Not everything you write about will manifest straightaway; some things take time. What I have come to understand about Scripting is that your success in what you will manifest is dependent on how aligned you are with it. If you truly believe in the words you write coming to form – then you will absolutely bring about what it is you desire.

Take that first step and write your own Script today. It doesn't have to be written in a fancy notebook – plain white paper will do. What's important is that it is handwritten – there is a real sense of power when you physically write out your desires. Most importantly don't hold yourself back. Write down *everything* that you desire - not just what you think is 'realistic'. Then make time every day to read your Script and to allow yourself to feel the emotions you would feel if that was your life *now*.

In your day-to-day life be open to the inspired thoughts that come your way, be open to the people that you may meet and new opportunities that present themselves.

Review your script after a couple of months and write down what has manifested for you, and then go ahead and write a refreshed one. I guarantee that if you have been completely open to this process and have enough faith and belief – you will be surprised at how much has manifested into form.

This technique is proof if ever you needed it of the individual power we have over our lives.

4. A 'FAILURE' IS ALWAYS A LESSON

There's a reason why I put 'Failure' in inverted commas. This word is loaded with so many negative emotions, but it really is all in how you perceive things. In life if you have had the courage and gumption to play full out for your dreams then chances are yes, sometimes things won't work out the way you had hoped. But is that really such a negative thing? Does it deserve the doom and gloom label of 'Failure'? Or is it that there is instead an incredible pearl of wisdom you can glean from that moment, that if you had been too fearful to live your life, you may have missed?

Now 'Failure' becomes empowering.

When I decided to start my business – with no entrepreneurial experience or background – people were keen to point out the risks associated with such an idea, disguised as always in the form of loving advice.

I had made the decision to walk away from what was perceived to be a secure career as a Police Officer to pursue my dream of a Vintage Tea Party and Catering business. "How will you pay your bills?" was just one of the questions regularly asked of me – in other words to translate – "There is a real chance your business won't be successful, so how will you financially survive?"

I can understand why so many people give up before they ever truly begin.

But there was a fire within me, a desire, an alignment to my dream and so I carried on. I'm so glad I did. I ran that business for four years, building it from boxes of vintage china into a six-figure operation. I opened a Tearoom premises, gained hundreds of clients – including high profile ones and repeat bookings - visited incredible places and won numerous awards including one from business magnate Theo Paphitis. I was one of Small Business Saturday's Top 100 Businesses and attended a private reception at 10 Downing Street - the home of the U.K Prime Minister - as well as receiving press coverage and radio appearances. After just one year of opening, I received the coveted TripAdvisor Certificate of Excellence for my Tearooms.

I never would have experienced any of this if I had given into the fear of 'Failure'.

Late 2017 though, I began to feel disillusioned with my life. On the surface business was booming. I was working non-stop often with multiple bookings on the same day and I had so much to be thankful for. But I was starting to feel resentment creeping up on me.

I would drive around to my various bookings on weekends and see people out having fun and I would wish that was me. I would be at home at night sending emails, updating the website and social media - wishing I could just switch off and relax. I had this incredible Tearoom yet I felt tied – the financial obligations of having staff, having a premises with all its associated responsibilities coupled with this deep feeling within that I had made a mistake in making my business a formal Partnership. All of this was starting to make me yearn for a different life.

In January 2018 I became certain that a different direction was what I desired for my life. That meant walking away from my business, relationships and life that I knew. On the one hand I was deliriously excited for the possibilities yet on the other I felt like I was 'Failing' because I was turning my back on all that I had worked so hard to build. But you know when you know and my mind was set.

A few months after I had started my new life and had ended my part in my business Partnership – I learnt that the business I had created had ceased to trade. I crumbled. I felt a complete and utter 'Failure'.

For the best part of 2019 I battled with feelings of shame and guilt. I had built something so successful and had walked away with nothing really to show for it all but memories. To know it was no more broke my heart. I became bound in invisible chains, holding myself back from pursuing any of my passions of sharing my story and helping others, because I felt like I had 'Failed'. I felt entirely responsible.

That experience was a turning point for me. I realised I had to start looking for the lessons rather than just focusing on the pain. Lessons after all are the greatest blessings.

So what were my lessons from this experience? Well I learnt that to follow your heart and passion is one of the most important things you can do. Not everybody will understand your choices and decisions but honestly that is okay - your dream is yours for a reason.

I learnt that you can never be responsible for the decisions of others and that there is no shame if things don't work out exactly as you had planned. Every perceived 'set-back' is really a stepping stone in the right direction. It's so important to feel pride for your journey - all of it - even the parts where you feel you made endless mistakes. For everything is a learning experience and you evolve and progress so much on the back of it.

If something isn't going well in your life and you feel like you have 'Failed', allow yourself time to feel your emotions – this is important – but then stand right back up, dust yourself down and look for the lessons. Look for the personal growth that can come on the back of this, look for the new opportunities. Look for the ways in which you can improve your life.

Nothing is ever really a 'Failure', just a lesson for us to learn. However hard that lesson may be, what you take from that will always lead to something even more beautiful.

* * *

5. YOU TAKE YOU, WHEREVER YOU GO

I learnt this lesson the most as I embarked on my new life in Italy. Once the buzz and excitement of espressos and sunshine had settled – I was left with the same uneasy feelings I had felt whilst living back in the U.K. I realised then that it doesn't matter how your environment changes – you will always be with you.

This is such a powerful lesson to learn because we often place so much attention on others that we neglect ourselves. Except ourselves are all we truly have – it's the most important, significant relationship in our lives.

People come and go into our experience, providing various levels of enrichment or learning but ultimately it is how we treat ourselves that will impact the life you lead. If you aren't feeling good with who you are inside, it doesn't matter what beauty may surround you – you will only see the negatives.

Embarking on a journey of personal development has been a game changer for me. This journey has evolved from 2014 when I first learnt about the Law of Attraction and the powerful book, *'The Secret'*, to now in 2020, where I am ever more aware of the power of our thoughts and the importance of loving yourself and healing.

Committing to creating a healthy, loving relationship with yourself means accepting those parts of you that you're not so happy with and doing the personal development work to improve yourself and your life.

It's not about putting a plaster on your wound and hoping that's going to be enough to heal it. You've got to tend to that wound, clean it and look after it, for it to recover.

Making a commitment to do the work on yourself, to uncover those limiting, self-sabotaging beliefs and discover tools and techniques to overcome them, is one of the most powerful things you can do. To fill your mind with content that is going to elevate you, to make lifestyle choices which are going to empower you and to decide that you are making *you* a priority is when things will start to change for you.

That is when the goodness you've been seeking from life, will reveal itself.

❋ ❋ ❋

6. LISTEN TO THOSE WHO WALK THEIR TALK

I t's natural for people to have opinions and want to offer their advice to you. That's the way of life. It's your choice though as to whose words you listen to.

When I relocated to Italy I felt as though I achieved a lot in a short space of time – gaining employment, my residency, healthcare, the conversion of my driving licence, opening a bank account, getting an Italian phone number, getting my Italian identity card and learning to move around independently as much as possible. The one thing that took a little longer to get used to was learning Italian – which makes what I did achieve even more incredible, considering I could barely communicate!

At the time of writing this book I've been living in Italy

for 18 months and I am now ready to embark on my language learning journey. A few months ago, I started to become aware of people's opinions about this. Some people thought that really by now I should know Italian whilst others believed that if *they* had relocated to another country, *they* would know the language by now. As harsh as those opinions sounded, I couldn't help but wonder if there was some truth in them.

Deep down I had bought into the limiting beliefs that it's more difficult for an adult to learn another language, I allowed myself to think there must be something wrong with me....until one day the switch went off. All those people who were quick to offer me their opinions hadn't achieved anything close to what I had achieved in my life – so why on earth was I listening to them?!

It's very easy for people to freely offer their opinions and beliefs but until you have lived life like the person you want to give advice to, how can you constructively help that person? The answer is you can't.

You need to listen to those people that have walked the path you want to tread, those people who have overcome the struggles that you may be facing right now and achieved what it is they desired. Those people may not be anybody you directly know. They can easily be someone you follow on social media, that doesn't matter.

What does matter is that you become extremely selective over whose advice you listen to. Please don't ever give your power away to a person who simply doesn't know what it's like to walk in your shoes.

Advice when coupled with love, compassion and experience are some of the best words you'll ever hear. Everything else is just background noise.

7. COMFORT ZONE VS GROWTH ZONE

L ying in a hospital bed in Palermo, Italy over Christmas of 2019, having reached my rock bottom, I had a decision to make. Was I going to remain in Italy or was it time to throw in the towel and return to the U.K? Turning to my phone for some sort of guidance, I came across an incredible post on Instagram from Mel Robbins, where she talked about Comfort Zones and Growth Zones.

Comfort Zones are often spoken about and they relate to those parts of our lives where we feel secure and comfortable. It's a sense of familiarity, a routine, something we know inside out. Comfort Zones may feel good on the surface but deep down we can never grow from a place like this. If we stay in our Comfort Zone, we ultimately become stagnant.

Growth Zones on the other hand often feel extremely uncomfortable. They push us out of our normality and what feels safe, into brand new experiences. From those new experiences are where we learn the most about ourselves. They are where we come alive and flourish.

It was immediately clear to me when I read that post what my decision would be.

The U.K was my Comfort Zone – the country of my birth, the home of my memories – a place where I easily knew my way around and where language wasn't a barrier.

Italy on the other hand was my Growth Zone. A place which everyday challenged me in different ways – from learning how to communicate to adapting to a new culture and complete change in lifestyle. A place where I was rebuilding my life from the ground up.

As much as I felt like I was underneath the rocks in that moment – I knew that if I returned to the U.K, it would become a huge regret of mine not to have followed through with my dream. Which is why in that moment lying in that hospital bed, feeling scared, with two drips in my arm and a whole lot of shame flowing through my body, I started to listen to my inner voice. That inner voice was telling me to stay in Italy. Feeling that this would ultimately help to heal me, even if right there and then I couldn't see how, I made that decision.

In the trickiest moments in our lives it's easy to want to stick in our Comfort Zone – much like a child clings onto a favourite toy for reassurance. Yet in our challenges and moments of pain are where we as humans can learn the most about ourselves and truly transform.

It's in those Growth Zone moments where when we embrace what is happening around us – even though it may feel extremely scary – a certainty will eventually emerge. Know this – that feeling of certainty marks the beginning of your rising.

"Yesterday I was clever so I wanted to change the world. Today I am wise so I am changing myself."

RUMI

8. THE LIFE CHANGING MAGIC OF TAPPING

T o make positive change in our lives requires us to be open to tools and techniques that can help us.

Emotional Freedom Technique (otherwise known as Tapping) is one of the most effective techniques I know of, to clear the limiting blocks and beliefs that hold us back from living our best lives.

I first discovered Tapping a couple of years ago via Brad Yates on his YouTube channel and I was instantly intrigued. Based on the principles of acupuncture, you tap gently on your body's energy meridian points on your face and upper body – whilst talking out loud what the block, limiting belief or sadness that is within you, that you are wanting to release.

The combination of both talking out loud what you are wanting to release coupled with the tapping action, shifts and clears through stagnant energy that you are holding onto in your body.

It's simple, painless and at worse may leave you feeling tired or a little nauseous as you clear through and release all that negative energy from within. The tears, burps and yawns you may also experience whilst doing this are a fantastic sign that it is working and that you are making space for more empowering thoughts.

Some of the things you Tap on, you may not feel instant relief from. A lot of the limiting beliefs and blocks we have are ingrained within us and have been present for a long time and so a few rounds of Tapping will be needed. Other things you Tap on, you will feel an instant shift.

Once you've Tapped out what you want to release, then it's time to Tap in and reinforce positive, empowering messages about yourself and your life. The results are incredible.

I recommend watching some Brad Yates' videos on YouTube and Gala Darling's too, so that you can follow along, know where to Tap and know what to say. Then when you are comfortable, you can create your own free-flowing Tapping routine whenever and wherever you want.

This technique is a daily part of my life and has helped me to overcome confidence issues and feelings of shame, guilt and unworthiness.

Give it a go today – see what it can do for you too.

9. STEER CLEAR OF NEGATIVITY & GOSSIP

I t's become the norm in our society to bond with others by sharing negative news and gossip. There are countless magazine titles, newspaper columns and internet sites filled with salacious stories about celebrities, all designed to get us talking and judging. In the workplace it's an addictive habit to talk about other colleagues. On social media people come together to share their woes.

I'm not going to be the person to say that you will always be a ray of sunshine or that you are never going to be triggered by somebody. What I will say is that whenever I have felt the need to talk badly about others, it has always left me feeling shit. Why? Because it's all coming from a low vibrational energy.

The same with being negative. Now to be clear – I'm

not talking about someone who is feeling depressed or low. If you know somebody who is feeling depressed or low, then I cannot stress enough the importance of being there for them and listening, protecting your own energy in the process. As we all know if our own cup isn't full, we cannot give or be of help to another. What I'm talking about are the times when people are negative for the sake of being negative and stubbornly refuse to look at things a different way.

Being negative in this way and sharing gossip may feel good in the moment but in the long run it is doing nothing for your dreams or your energy.

When you start to do the work on improving yourself and your mindset, your eyes suddenly become open to the negativity and gossip surrounding you. It's almost as if the blinkers have been removed. It is from this space though that your choices in life become glaringly clear.

❈ ❈ ❈

You can choose who you follow or unfollow on social media.

We often underestimate just how much our mindset and mood are impacted by social media and the subsequent effect it has on our mental health. Which is why being intentional with the people we follow and the people we unfollow is incredibly important. For me I chose to leave some Expat groups on Facebook which were disempowering me with people's constant negative experiences of life in Italy – the complete opposite to my own. Rather than let my own view become tarnished, I hit the exit button.

* * *

You can choose who you surround yourself with.

There is that famous saying that talks about how you are the best of the five people, that you spend the most time with. That's quite a sobering thought. If your friends like to moan and complain then either do activities with them that limit the opportunity for this or better still, start to seek out more like-minded companions. Having people in our lives who uplift and elevate us, is so incredibly powerful and will inspire you to want to achieve great things.

* * *

You can choose to change the conversation if those around you start to gossip.

This subtle action sends a huge, neon flashing sign of a message, that gossiping just isn't for you. It also tends to stop it right in its tracks. Gossiping after all, loves company.

* * *

You can choose in any given moment to look for the positive aspects in a situation.

If life isn't unfolding as you had planned, see if you can glean something good from it. As I was editing this book, the worldwide Coronavirus Pandemic struck, and Italy went into country-wide lockdown. Suddenly, it became very evident that life was never going to be quite the same again. Feelings of fear and uncertainty hung heavy in the air and with future plans dashed, life became about living in the moment. It was very accepting and normal to want to cling onto the negativity and sadness of the situation. It was also possible to find some goodness.

I chose to see this enforced time at home as a blessing – a chance to reconnect with myself, with my dreams and remotely with others. A chance to be still and present. This was an opportunity for us all collectively to really look at the way we were living our lives and commit to making empowering changes. Even with the deaths and the tears, there was still a way to find hope.

✳ ✳ ✳

You can choose to fill your mind with inspiring and nourishing content.

An evening with a life changing book such as *'The Alchemist'*, does far more for me than watching a violent film on Netflix.

> *As William Wordsworth once said, "Your mind is the garden, your thoughts are the seeds; the harvest can either be flowers or weeds."*

❋ ❋ ❋

The sooner you realise that everything in life is a choice, the sooner you will release yourself from the low vibrational shackles that we intentionally place ourselves in. It takes time to learn to protect your own vibration from what is going on around you, but it is time very well spent.

Our vibrations always reflect back to us the events that unfold in our lives and so by becoming intentional over who we spend time with, the words we speak and what we fill our mind with, will have a very powerful impact on the quality of our experiences.

❋ ❋ ❋

"Don't be satisfied with stories, how things have gone with others. Unfold your own myth."

RUMI

10. YOUR STORY IS YOUR OWN

No two people's lives or experiences are the same. We have different perceptions, beliefs and outlooks. We have different expectations, opinions and priorities. We each have our own individual quirks and patterns of behaviour – which is why you need to exercise caution if you feel influenced by somebody else's opinion or experience.

Take a website such as TripAdvisor – this is designed to help you in deciding where to go, based on the reviews of others. Now there are many positives for this, but it is about keeping an open mind. Some reviews may be inaccurate and some may have hidden agendas. Imagine if you missed out on eating at an incredible restaurant because you listened to a couple of negative reviews, from diners who maybe wanted to sabotage the success of the business, due to jealousy. Trust me, this happens.

It's exactly the same when it comes to our dreams and our own lives. People are always ready to give advice and offer their opinions (sometimes when it's not even asked for!). It is however down to us what if anything, we choose to accept.

When I decided to move to Italy you should have heard the things people would say to me. I was informed that it was impossible to find work in Southern Italy - that even Italians left the country for better career prospects. I was told that the bureaucracy was a nightmare and that in a nutshell everything would be *really fucking difficult.*

If it wasn't for the fact that I had this deep connection and alignment with moving, I may very well have ended up listening to these fear-based opinions and what an absolute shame that would have been. For my experiences ended up being nothing like what people spoke about.

I secured three job interviews (the first job interviews I had ever had outside of the U.K and, the first job interviews I had had in 10 years!). I accepted one of those jobs, in a role that lit my heart up and ticked every expectation I had wanted from my new employment.

I easily and effortlessly sorted out the administration side of moving to Italy – and even though sometimes I had to make a repeat visit to the same office – the bureaucracy was nowhere near as bad as people had said it would be.

I'm sure some people have struggled with all of this and I'm not downplaying that at all. I'm just saying that somebody else's story doesn't have to become yours.

You can tell yourself a different story. Your story is your own.

When people share their experiences, you have to remember that included in them are that person's individual blend of beliefs and behaviours – some of which may not be that beneficial to you at all. It is super important that you do what lights you up, even and especially if those people around you want to tell you it's impossible or the worst decision ever. Those doubts are really the other person's own fears being expressed and so if you take those opinions on board, you are also taking on that other person's blocks and beliefs too.

You are the creator of your own life. You can choose how you want your life to be and the experiences you have. Take advice when it resonates. If it doesn't tune out and stay aligned with what feels good to you. Don't let somebody else write the story that is yours.

11. ONWARDS

You've probably heard before the importance of taking teeny, tiny steps forward even when things feel incredibly tough. There's a reason behind this and it's called forward momentum.

When we are in the thick of a situation and everything feels hopeless, it's easy to want to give up and succumb to feeling shit or give in to self-sabotaging behaviours. Trust me when I say that this does nothing for you and only keeps you feeling stuck. True progression is gained through forward momentum.

When I was going through my break-up, I felt every negative emotion possible. I was so frustrated because I knew about mindset and the power of our thoughts, yet I just couldn't seem to shake it. I allowed myself to spiral slowly downwards until I had that hospital moment in Palermo.

All through this I didn't know how I was going to move forward – I felt stuck in a place of tears and heartache. As I'm writing this now just weeks later, I am in a more empowered, strong place. Everything I was fearing is resolving itself and showing to me that I have nothing to worry about. I am more mentally prepared for my solo life here in Italy and I've taken more steps towards my dreams and goals in the last few weeks than I did in the last year. So how did I go from a place of utter despair to one of strength and empowerment? By taking teeny, tiny steps forward.

The biggest lesson this whole experience taught me was that I wasn't loving myself anywhere near enough. So, some of my steps forward focused on listening to incredible podcasts and YouTube videos, from people who uplifted me and spoke to my soul with their incredible words of wisdom. I made Tapping a daily practise to clear through my old blocks and patterns of behaviour. I got clear on my dreams and goals and started to put into action what previously had just been words. I started saying 'Yes' to life more, even if I didn't have all the answers at the time. I read books that blew my mind.

These were all tiny incremental movements, but they were carrying me forward. Over time I became stronger and started to see things a hell of a lot differently.

Don't be that person sitting there lamenting on how life used to be. You can't go back and undo anything. What you can do though is make the small changes, focus on what you desire and move forward.

Onwards

* * *

If it's a loving relationship you desire, know that doing the work on being the best, most independent version of yourself, is going to mean that whatever comes on the back of single life, will be fresh and exciting.

Onwards.

* * *

If you are tempted to revisit the past – remember times and people change. Nostalgia is a funny thing – in many ways it feels safe and comforting. It was these feelings of nostalgia that led me to re-apply for a job at a famous Toyshop in London, where I had enjoyed some fun working times a few years prior. When I started working there again though – it was nothing like I had lovingly remembered it to be. I found myself feeling increasingly unhappy and quit a short time after. When we try to recreate a moment from our past, we are forgetting that we are not necessarily that same person anymore.

Onwards.

* * *

If it's your finances that are stressing you out – work

on telling yourself a different, more empowering story. Take the action – look for new jobs or opportunities that can bring in the money. Read the books, do the Tapping and start releasing the lack and scarcity that is blocking you from true abundance. Be open to the possibilities.

Onwards.

❋ ❋ ❋

If it's your health that has you feeling stuck – look for improvements, you can make to your lifestyle. Educate yourself through books and the internet on alternative therapies and dietary choices. Do the Tapping to release the fear.

If a Doctor gives you a scary diagnosis, know that you are more powerful than those words. I know people who were told they had just a few short months left to live and carried on strong for years. Your thoughts are that intentional. It's when we give up on ourselves that our bodies shut down soon after.

Onwards.

❋ ❋ ❋

Whatever you do, remember it's always, always about heading onwards

12. DON'T BREAK YOUR OWN PROMISES

How many times have you caught yourself saying the fateful words, "I'll start tomorrow – I promise." Whether it's a fitness goal or work on your business – if you find yourself backtracking and quitting on your promises, there's something deeper at work here. That something being fear.

Writing this book, I found myself uttering those words countless times. I would easily have another glass of wine, spend an hour scrolling through YouTube or take a siesta but when it came to making progress on my dreams and writing – I found myself constantly breaking my own promises. I would waste the pockets of time I was blessed with, I would procrastinate and I would continuously re-read parts of the book I had already written, meaning I would end up writing only a fraction of what I was capable of. Until I finally woke up. I realised that this was a promise that I was making to myself and....... breaking. And whilst it might have felt good in the moment to do something different, I knew the days were unfolding and if I carried on this way, another year would pass by with nothing to show for my dreams.

But why would I do this to myself? When I took the time to really answer that question, I realised that it was solely fear based. I had fears about being so open and vulnerable with my writing, fears about whether I was good enough and fears over other people's perceptions. It was fear that had me in a headlock.

Whenever we do something new or we follow a passion or dream, there is a huge element of change involved. Change is scary. Change takes us out of our comfort zones into new experiences. As our brains just want to protect us, we find ways to resist the changes and stay in a space of feeling safe. We procrastinate. We make excuses. We break our promises. Life stays the same. We never fulfil the potential that is within each of us. Our dreams and desires stay just that. Nothing comes to fruition.

The promises we make to ourselves really are one of the most important. For if we cannot be true with ourselves, then how much do we truly value our dreams and our desires? And more to the point, how much do we truly value the person we are?

To break through this, you need to uncover the hidden

fears that are holding you back, so that the intention behind the promise you are making yourself, can shine through.

* * *

If the promise to yourself is to start your own business – the fear wants to paralyse you with all the associated risks. The intention behind your promise wants to remind you that you are doing this to create a better life for yourself.

* * *

If the promise to yourself is to become fitter – the fear wants to paralyse you with how difficult it's going to be. The intention behind your promise wants to remind you that you are doing this to have a stronger, healthier body.

* * *

When you clear the fog of fear, the power of your intention becomes illuminated.

Tapping is my go-to technique for moving from a place of fear to a place of love. It helps to shift what are sometimes incredibly subtle beliefs, that are preventing you from fulfilling your commitment to yourself.

Once you've cleared through them, you can replace the fear with more loving, empowered thoughts. From this place, you'll find yourself more committed than ever to staying true to your own promises.

13. WHAT IS MEANT FOR YOU, WILL NEVER PASS YOU BY

T his is a beautiful lesson because when we don't get what we had wanted in life, it's easy to feel despondent. The thing to remember however is that when something doesn't work out for us it's usually a blessing and what is right for us, normally always follows.

There are so many examples I have of this from my own life.

* * *

When I was looking for a commercial premises for my Tearoom, I was set on it being in Brighton, a seaside city in the U.K that I spent a lot of time in. I found one but the location wasn't really ideal – the footfall was pretty non-existent. Still, I fell in love with wanting a Tearoom there and pursued it but it never worked out. Looking back, I can see just what a blessing that was. The location I did end up opening a Tearoom in, was central on a High Street and about thirty minutes outside of Brighton itself. I didn't end up having to pay business rates and I didn't have any identical vintage themed businesses in the area.

What is meant for you, will never pass you by.

❀ ❀ ❀

When I was in the process of moving to Italy – I fell in love with an apartment which overlooked the sea and had an enormous sun-drenched balcony which wrapped around the outside of the building. The interior however was a shell – I would have had to fit a kitchen, new bathroom suite and get the electrics in order as well as furnish it. It would have been a big job and costly too but I was besotted.

At the time I was still running my business in the U.K and part of the process was to prove my income. However, the document the Italian estate agents required for this was no longer used in the U.K. Needless to say, the delay in all of this meant I lost the apartment to somebody else. I was gutted. A year later and through someone I knew, I found out about a beautiful brand new fully furnished apartment that was very central to everything. It was perfect and divine and cost less per month than the other one I had loved!

What is meant for you, will never pass you by.

❋ ❋ ❋

When I joined an online Female Entrepreneur Group and elected to be paired up with an accountability partner, the incredible woman I met – Fiona – I later discovered wasn't originally meant to be paired with me at all. Her initial pairing hadn't worked out. Well that was an incredible blessing because we have become a real part of each other's lives and every day commit to a beautiful morning practice together, where we capture our gratitude and desires both for the day ahead and for our futures.

What is meant for you, will never pass you by.

❋ ❋ ❋

When I went to buy my first car through someone I knew – my friend who knew a thing or two about mechanics came along to double check it. Well it turned out the car, which was already quite old, wasn't safe to drive and would probably have conked out two miles down the road. I left empty handed and disappointed. A few months later I bought my first car – which was just three years old – and in immaculate condition. That car served me well and was a dream to drive until it was time to upgrade a couple of years later.

What is meant for you, will never pass you by.

❊ ❊ ❊

I'm sure if you reflect there are moments in your life where things haven't gone exactly as you had planned. Yet when you look back in the end, a greater blessing came your way.

Trust and have faith that everything is always happening for your highest good and remember what is meant for you - although it may take a little while to arrive - will never, ever pass you by.

❊ ❊ ❊

14. FORCED UPGRADES

Sometimes we procrastinate in life. We talk about doing things and then stop. We consider changing something and then retreat. We desire something different but take no action. This is when the Universe steps in with what I call Forced Upgrades.

Forced Upgrades are the times when we are forced to buy the new and improved product or make the lifestyle change or step outside of our comfort zones because we have no other choice but to. Only when we reflect back, do we see the goodness contained in those moments.

❊ ❊ ❊

I loved my first car, I really did. It got me from A to B as well as to all the mobile bookings I had with my business. As my business grew though, I found myself desiring something bigger that would easily fit everything in that I needed. It stayed a thought though and I didn't take any action on it. A few months later and my car was due its MOT. I took it to my local garage to check it over beforehand and it turned out that there were numerous things wrong with it, including the fact it would need a new exhaust and tyres. Now this car was a few years old now and I had recently spent a fair bit of money on a new clutch, so I had a decision to make. Was I going to continue to pour money into it or was it now time to upgrade to something bigger? Forced Upgrade noted. I decided to trade in my car and get the bigger car I desired.

* * *

I thought I would always be a Police Officer – it is after all often perceived as a career for life – and the amount of training you go through warrants this. Six years in and I was happy. However, budget cuts struck and Officers were moved around to plug staffing gaps because recruitment was frozen. I had a specific skill set which was needed and which meant I was moved from frontline policing which I loved, to being in a call centre environment which depleted me. I was told the move would be for two years and then I could return to policing the streets – which is what I had joined for. However, the world of policing is a rapid one and I knew how outdated and rusty I would feel after those two years. Forced Upgrade noted. This move got me desiring more control over my working life and led me to start thinking about becoming an Entrepreneur. A few months later I left the Police to become a full-time business owner.

❊ ❊ ❊

When my relationship ended with my 'Earth Angel', I was left feeling bemused. I had thought everything was just fine and nothing had been communicated to me to tell me otherwise. Moving to a brand-new country where I didn't speak the language meant that I had relied heavily on him to set my life up and for my day-to-day errands. I was talking a lot about things I was wanting to do – but I was just talking. We were doing everything together and I was not being as independent as I usually was. I felt a little stagnant. Forced Upgrade noted. The separation revealed to me my inner strength. It renewed the independent streak in me and empowered me to start this book and to start doing the things I had previously never acted on. It shone the light on the healing work I needed to do within so that I would value and love myself unconditionally. It exposed how I always looked externally for validation and approval. In short, this separation transformed me into the best, brightest version of myself that I could have asked for.

❊ ❊ ❊

Forced Upgrades often feel difficult or painful in the moment. There is however such beauty contained within them, when you take the time to look back.

I'm a big believer that life happens for us and not to us. With this in mind, Forced Upgrades to me are filled with the best intentions for us. It's the Universe's way of showing up for you, at a time when you just aren't able to show up for yourself.

* * *

15. YOU ARE
NEVER ALONE

Being an only child for the best part I loved. As I grew older though I wondered how different my life would have been if I had had brothers and sisters to share it with. Friendships in my life ebbed and flowed as I evolved and grew and there were times when I felt like I didn't have a huge support network of friends who I could really count on. I started to have moments where I really felt alone.

Loneliness creeps up on you when you least expect it. You could be out having a coffee and look across to a table full of friends laughing and joking and suddenly the empty seat across from you, is as bold as day. Perhaps it's when you want to go and do something but have no-one to go with – suddenly you feel full of anxiety that people are going to judge you and think you are a loner.

Moving to Italy I became acutely aware of how close-knit families are here and how friendships are an integral part of life. Everyone is so friendly that often strangers would spark up conversations but not being able to speak the language at the time, meant I instantly isolated myself. When my relationship ended, I found myself questioning how I would meet new people and how I would maintain our mutual friendships. I started to get mild panic attacks at the thought of taking a drink in a busy bar by myself or going out by myself in the evening, because of what others would think. I was mentally putting myself in a prison.

The truth is we are never alone. And I mean this. Even when I was lying in that hospital bed in Palermo, I was able to turn to the tribe of people I follow on Instagram and YouTube to help elevate me. I realised that these people I may never physically get to meet in person but that didn't matter. They and their bad-ass words of wisdom were there for me when I needed it the most.

Physical connection is incredibly important, but it isn't the be all and end all of combating loneliness. Building your tribe of like-minded, inspiring people - whether it be on one of the social media platforms or through an online group – can be super effective at shaking us out of our lonelier moments, without having somebody physically next to you.

Never was this more evident than during the Coronavirus Pandemic, which forced Italy along with many other countries around the world, into a state of complete lockdown. Suddenly faced with weeks in our homes, unable to socialise – loneliness became even more prevalent, especially with those who lived on their own. It was in this moment that being online helped people feel more connected than ever before.

To overcome feelings of loneliness it's important to stop comparing yourself to others. The truth is we never really know the full picture of what is happening in somebody else's life. Social media can lure us into this comparison trap but really social media is simply a carefully curated view of the life somebody else is living. The edited parts. The likes you get, the number of friends or followers you have – none of that matters. The truth is that out of the hundreds of friends you may have on Facebook or the thousands of followers on Instagram – how many of them are a real part of your daily life? How many of them would be there for you if you needed it?

Stop telling yourself that it gets harder to meet new people and make friends, as we get older. Our sub-conscious mind never makes us a liar and so if this is what we believe, our brains will continuously look for evidence of this in our own lives. Our thoughts are that powerful.

Instead start getting out there more – even if it makes you feel physically sick. It's all about stepping out of our comfort zones. Take yourself to dinner, go get a drink and go head to the art show you've really wanted to go to. Be open to the people around you – stop comparing and wondering what they are thinking – and just enjoy being in that moment. When you've done it once or twice, it won't feel anywhere near as scary.

Do the Tapping to clear through the blocks and beliefs that keep you feeling isolated and lonely. Ultimately get some goals and dreams to focus on – because when you are busy doing you, suddenly you don't have time to dwell on who may or may not be around you.

Take this time to grow and flourish and soon enough your life will start to feel fuller and resemble beautiful, bright new beginnings.

16. GRATITUDE IS AS ESSENTIAL AS WATER

Yes, even when life is tough and in fact especially in those moments, there is always something you can find to be thankful for.

You made it to another day. You have a roof over your head and a bed at night. You can see. You can hear. You can smell. You can taste. You can read. You have your health. You have the complete power to change your life at any moment.

The fact remains that gratitude is an absolute life changer.

We are almost programmed as a society to focus and dwell on the negatives in our lives. It's those vulnerabilities that advertisers' prey on, when trying to sell their latest products to us. It's what keeps us feeling stuck. It's what keeps us feeling like we are not enough and that we never have enough.

Instead when we turn our attention to what we can be thankful for, suddenly everything shifts.

If everything in your life seems to be falling apart right now, it's going to be trickier to see the good than if everything is rosy – so start small. Keep your gratitude general to begin with – maybe it's the fact the sun is out today, or you can see pretty flowers from your window – starting this way helps you to get used to the practice of gratitude, until you feel able to be more specific with the good things in your own life.

Journaling is a fabulous way to record gratitude or if writing isn't your thing, recording voice notes of gratitude on your phone is another great way. Having a record of what you are grateful for, helps massively in those moments when all you can see is the darkness.

There's so much we take for granted in our lives, without ever really taking the time to feel appreciation. Gratitude stops us, centres us in the present moment and opens our eyes to the goodness of what we do have.

When we choose to look at life from this way – actively looking for the good – we start to see more of that reflected to us. That is the power of being grateful.

17. HEARTACHE IS A HEALER

I started writing this book on the back of the completion of the romantic relationship I had been in, with the man who I lovingly refer to as my 'Earth Angel'. Now I'm 36 years old and I've been in a fair few long-term relationships, but I took the end of this one so badly, that I realised it had to be happening for my personal growth and evolution. So, I decided to do some reflection.

I took it back, way, way back and realised that every single person I had had a romantic connection with over the years – just hadn't been right for me. Every single one! They had either been emotionally unavailable or not available at all, all about their own personal gain or had their own underlying issues which manifested in the form of control and anger. Which begs the question really – why the hell did I even go there?!

Well here's the answer I know now and only now – and

it pains me to admit it – I just didn't love myself enough to want to be alone or value my self-worth enough to realise I could do better. I saw being in a relationship as some sort of status symbol and that if you were single then it meant that you weren't deemed good enough and that there must be something wrong with you. What utter crap.

I literally hopped from long-term relationship to long-term relationship hardly spending any time truly single and alone.

I realised that I had to do the work on my self-worth and on being in a loving relationship with myself, because the alternative was simply unhealthy. The alternative was to keep on hurting myself, to keep on denying myself a chance to experience a healthy, happy, harmonious relationship with another person that was full of love.

It's easy to buy into the premise that heartache is a real melancholy experience – a time where you feel shit and beat up on yourself about what went wrong. That's such a waste and incredibly disempowering. Of course, it hurts but as with anything in life, the experience is all in how you perceive it.

Heartache can be the biggest healing lesson you've ever had – it can be your opportunity to evolve and become a stronger, more empowered person, regardless of what happened. This time of contrast can help you to get crystal clear on what you desire from a romantic partner and help you to form new non-negotiables about what you will and won't accept in the future. It's also the time to get comfortable with your own company, so that you stop placing your worth and validation in the hands of another.

Heartache is a necessary part of life but don't let it knock your ability to love fully in the future. When I'm in a romantic relationship I love with every piece of my heart – I will always be this way. Anything less just isn't true to me. It's just now my heart is that little bit wiser.

"Comparison is the thief of joy."

THEODORE ROOSEVELT

18. CUT OUT COMPARISON

It was Sunday afternoon in Italy. The streets were deserted, the smell of incredible food filled the air and sitting on my balcony, I could hear the distant chatter of families gathered for lunch. I was alone and I had no plans for the rest of the day. Right then it felt like everyone else was living a better life than me.

Comparison creeps up on us like the flu. Whether we are triggered by something in our daily lives or by an advertisement we see – the feeling is the same. It's shit.

The thing with comparison though is that it is viewed solely from our perspective. This sole perception of a situation often feeds us with negative, disempowering stories that do nothing to serve us and are completely artificial. For how often do we truly know what happens behind closed doors or how someone is really coping with a situation, deep down?

The most empowering way to navigate comparison is to turn the attention you are placing on other people and their lives, back onto yourself.

That Sunday I chose to do just that. I placed my attention back onto this book that I wanted to finish so I could share it with the world. Back onto the relaxing day that lay ahead where I didn't have to go anywhere or do anything. Back on to the time I had to do some Tapping, to listen to things that uplifted me and to do what made me feel good. Suddenly it didn't matter so much what everyone else was doing.

It's not just other people's lives that we compare ourselves to but also how others look. Body image is such a sensitive subject and one which isn't helped by the idealised images projected by the media of the 'perfect' body.

For a long time, I wasn't happy with my body. I gained weight from being in an unhappy relationship and I didn't wear a bikini for years. When I transformed my life and moved to Italy, the weight dropped off and I am now the skinniest I have ever been. But get this – even at a UK size 8/10 with not an ounce of fat to my name, I still have my body hang-ups. Which is why comparison is such a dangerous game to play. You just never know what is going through someone's mind or how they feel about themselves.

Be super mindful of your thoughts and when you find them creeping to other people in contrast to you, remember we are all on our own individual paths. All on our own unique journeys. No two people's lives will be the same because we all have our own lessons to learn and experiences to have.

Stop placing everyone else on a pedestal in relation to you and focus on what lights you up as a person. Focus on what you desire to achieve in your life. Work on building a tribe of high vibe people who elevate you and remind you of your wonder, the next time you find yourself looking at others and beating up on what isn't going right for you.

Learn to treat comparison as a signpost to your own life's desires as opposed to something more toxic. If you feel triggered that everyone else is in a relationship apart from you, work on the relationship you have with yourself and on living your best life. Working on being the very best version of yourself will naturally make you more magnetic to those that are right for you.

If it's your body that is your weakness, then how can you improve your feelings towards it – can you make more inspired food choices? Make a commitment to working out at the gym? Do some Tapping to release your blocks around your image?

When we take steps to improve ourselves we make more of an impact than looking at others ever will.

Like we cut certain foods out of our diet to become healthier – create a healthier mind by cutting out comparison. Your whole life will thank you for it.

✻ ✻ ✻

19. JOIN THOSE DOTS

I remember hearing the famous graduation speech which the late Steve Jobs gave at Stanford University in 2005. In it he spoke about 'connecting the dots' in understanding, when looking back, why events unfold in life the way they do.

I'm sure this is evident in your own life too. If it hadn't been for one scenario happening maybe you wouldn't have ended up doing what you do now or living where you do or knowing the people you do. It's very much a retrospective process but it provides us with the faith to know that everything always happens for our highest good, even if we cannot see it at the time.

I have many examples from my own life.

* * *

If I hadn't been moved to another department in the Police to plug staffing gaps, I wouldn't have left to become an Entrepreneur.

* * *

If I hadn't experienced life as an Entrepreneur, I don't think I ever would have had the courage to start my life over in a brand-new country.

* * *

If I hadn't started my life over in a brand-new country and experienced all that I had, I wouldn't be sitting here now writing this book.

* * *

It's all about joining those dots.

The thing that's so incredible when you join those dots is that you really come to understand why everything had to happen the way it did, so that you could be where and who you are today.

It's empowering to know that when life doesn't deliver the ice cream sundae with the cherry on top that you had asked for, it's because there's something way better that's on its way. Something more satisfying, something more enriching and something that is going to help you in becoming the best, most powerful version of yourself. Always. The Universe only trades up.

Even if what you are going through is incredibly tough and it's taking every ounce of you to put one step in front of another – keep the faith. This moment in your life will shape you into being strong, courageous and ultimately a force to be reckoned with.

I'm a big believer that life happens for us and not to us. This is essentially what joining those dots proves. Every circumstance, every scenario, every argument, every illness, every moment of stress, every tear, every broken heart – it's all a part of your life that is playing out to help you to be the best version of yourself possible.

It's one thing to get stuck in the tough times in our lives – it's quite another to view them as necessary dots, on the artistic masterpiece which is our life journey.

20. NETFLIX IS A DREAM STEALER

Now don't get me wrong. I'm not saying never watch TV or never do what you enjoy doing because you've got goals. No. What I'm saying is if you have dreams and goals, but you spend more time watching Netflix, than on taking any action towards what's really going to make a difference in your life – then honestly it becomes a dream stealer.

What's really happening when you are binge watching your favourite show rather than taking a small step towards your dream – is that you are procrastinating. Fear and procrastination are the best of friends. We procrastinate when we are entering new territory or doing something that we are simply not used to. The unknown of what we are doing builds in us a sense of fear and our brains, wired as they are to protect us, look for something else we can do instead to keep us feeling safe. Cue Netflix.

The thing with our dreams and goals is that they require attention and baby steps to make them happen. The time we spend on what isn't going to serve our future is time taken away from doing what can bring the life we desire into form. It's as simple as that.

Love yourself enough to want to make a daily commitment to your dreams and goals. If it's important enough to you, then this won't be an issue. If you're finding yourself making excuses, then you must ask yourself whether you do really want what you think you want.

As with anything, life reflects to us what we put in. If we take little steps towards our dreams and goals, every single day, then this builds forward momentum. Forward momentum brings you ever closer to that which you desire.

The next time you find yourself reaching mindlessly for the remote control – remember this - nothing is ever achieved in life through words alone. Go take some action. That is the difference between getting what you want and dreaming about it.

21. REJECTION IS PROTECTION

This is such a bitter pill to swallow because let's face it when you've been rejected, in that moment it feels like the worst thing that could ever happen. It doesn't matter if it's a romantic rejection, a career rejection, a friendship rejection – they all play into our deepest insecurities about whether we are good enough.

But what if instead of viewing rejection as this super negative, soul-destroying experience, we chose instead to see it as the Universe's way of protecting us? Sound too radical for you? Let's explore it a little more.

All of us have experienced rejection at some stage in our lives but have you ever taken the time to understand how your life evolved on the back of it? What new experiences emerged, what new people you met – which otherwise may never have come about? Writing this book has certainly made me reflect.

The rejection contained within my romantic relationship with my 'Earth Angel' – hurt like hell – but on the other side taught me so much. The Universe was protecting me because I needed to stop losing myself and become more independent. I needed to value my worth and love myself more – rather than placing that responsibility in the hands of another. I needed to remember why I had moved to Italy – it was never for the love of another; it was for re-discovering my own personal joy. I needed that rejection to shake me back to life.

✻ ✻ ✻

If you've been rejected for a job you've always wanted – you best believe that it's because the Universe has lined up something greater for you.

✻ ✻ ✻

If you've been rejected for finance – understand the Universe knows you can make the money you desire another way, one that doesn't involve the heavy burden of debt.

✻ ✻ ✻

If you've been rejected by your friends – rest assured

the right people will come into your life, who are more in alignment with who and where you are now.

* * *

It's all too easy to view rejection as this big bad wolf and make it mean we are not good enough. But, as you can see from just some of the examples above, it doesn't have to be that way at all. Once we have calmed our egos – the parts of ourselves that always like to be right – we can start to look at rejection with some clarity. We can even start to look at rejection as guidance. What falls away from our lives was never meant to remain and someday you will look back and understand exactly why.

For now though, if you are dealing with feelings of rejection, look for the protection contained within it. Was it really such an amazing job offer? The perfect relationship? The ideal friendship? I mean, really? Or deep down did you have your doubts that you had somehow glossed over? Were there things that you weren't entirely happy about?

I'm willing to bet that if you really do some soul searching, suddenly that rejection isn't going to look like such a bad thing after all.

22. FREEDOM THROUGH FORGIVENESS

Forgiveness is one of those things that divides so many people. You have those who embrace forgiveness as a way of freeing themselves from the emotional baggage of carrying resentments. On the flip side you have those who think to forgive is to show weakness and acceptance of the other person's actions. Personally, I just don't think enough of us realise what emotional chains we place ourselves in, when we hold onto the wrongs that others have done to us.

There's that famous saying that says holding onto resentments is like drinking poison and expecting the other person to die. Honestly, it's so true. You end up emotionally chained to the situation, projecting your unhealed pain onto others when the person who has wronged you has quite often moved on from that moment and is living their life. This is of course a lot easier to say than to do, especially if the person who has wronged you has done something particularly devastating. Even in those extremely difficult moments though, finding a way to forgive will set you free.

To forgive someone isn't to say that you agree with what they have done. It isn't accepting their behaviours or the hurt or pain they caused you. Forgiveness instead is an acknowledgement of all those feelings but then it is about realising that you can free yourself from them. It is about moving yourself into a place of peace.

I believe that the behaviours and actions we put out into the world will ultimately end up reflecting back to us. If we can learn to demonstrate forgiveness and grace towards others, then we open ourselves up to receiving the same.

But how do you learn to forgive?

This is a very individual experience, but below are some suggestions to try to help you with this process.

* * *

Writing is such a healing experience. To pour your pain and hurt into words on a page, is a form of release from within. You can direct your writing towards the person who has wronged you or you can generally talk about how it has made you feel. Once you have written down your feelings – find a physical way to demonstrate your detachment from them. Maybe you burn the paper you wrote on or maybe you shred it into tiny pieces and discard it in the rubbish.

The physical act of destroying what you have written sub-consciously breaks the bond that these emotions have held you in. Depending on the severity of the situation, this may be something you have to repeat a number of times – until the associated feelings begin to subside, until you can look back at the situation with less emotional charge. From this place you begin to free yourself, you begin to step into a space of forgiveness.

❈ ❈ ❈

Tapping is a tool to use to find your own way to forgiveness. Tap on the emotions and feelings you have toward your particular situation and then Tap in how you choose to want to see it instead. This will dismantle the negative emotional connections you have towards the person who has wronged you.

❈ ❈ ❈

Connect with empathy. This is probably one of the trickiest exercises to do, particularly if you have been deeply wounded. It is however very powerful –

especially if you know a little about the person who has hurt you. When we take ourselves into a space where we can recognise why people behave the way they do and put together the jigsaw pieces of their life – we move into empathy. Empathy is not about agreeing with the situation, but it is about moving towards an understanding of just why someone has hurt you. It removes us from our victim state – where we can only see the reaction it has caused in us and how powerless it may leave us feeling – to a more empowered position where we can start to find forgiveness.

In my own personal experience this has helped me greatly. One particular person who hurt me deeply in my past, had a challenging childhood and whilst I am a big believer that we can make our own choices for our lives, having empathy helped me to have more of an understanding as to why they behaved the way they did. It made it less about me.

❖ ❖ ❖

Speaking to a therapist or counsellor can also help you to process your emotions. Bottling up how we feel is the most damaging thing that we can do. Being able to speak through how you are feeling in a safe space can help greatly in moving yourself from a place of pain to one of forgiveness.

❖ ❖ ❖

Finding forgiveness is a journey and one that will look different to each and every one of us. It is however one of the most powerful and important acts we can do, in freeing ourselves from the hurtful actions and behaviours of others.

* * *

23. BE THE LIGHT

I remember hearing Bob Proctor once say, that if someone wrongs you in life you never need to worry, they will get their reward. I really resonated with this because he wasn't referencing revenge or any sort of low vibrational, negative reaction. What he was referring to is the way the Universe works – call it Karma or whatever you will – but essentially the way you treat others, will always reflect back to you.

It's interesting because when I think back to some of the people that wronged me in my past, over time things happened to them or they had situations to navigate, that without a doubt was their Karmic reward. I'm sure if you look back through your own life, you'll see evidence of this too.

I find it really empowering to remember these words because when we have been hurt or wronged, the associated negative emotions can keep us in a place of stagnation. We start to take things personally, we beat up on ourselves, we feel a mixture of anger and sadness.

But simply by remembering this statement, we can start to shift the energy. We can start to shine our light again. We can start to be the light in our life.

You are the most brilliant bright diamond. Never allow someone who may treat you like a pebble to affect your brilliance. Know your worth enough to walk away, with your head held high. Sometimes people for their own blocks, do not know how to handle something so exquisite. That is not your problem. You keep shining bright and the right people who appreciate your worth will soon follow.

We can never control or be responsible for the actions of others. That's the first thing to remember. What we CAN control though is our response to them. We always have a choice in any given moment how we are going to feel, regardless of what might be happening around us. We always have a choice as to how we respond, to what could be the biggest shit storm swirling around our ears. We always have a choice as to whether we dim our light in life, or we turn it up to max. We always have a choice.

Learning to shine your light bright, even when everything around you is falling apart, is one of the most challenging lessons we can learn but it is one of the most important. For there will always be contrast in life – situations that on the surface seem absolutely terrible – but if we can work through those times in a way which embraces the lessons that can be learnt and the personal growth that can be made, then we really start to evolve.

The Coronavirus Pandemic was one such example of how easy it could be to be sucked into the negativity and uncertainty of the moment. Some people believed that if you were being positive during this time, then it meant you were dismissing all those who tragically lost their lives or whose lives would be heavily impacted due to the lockdown. I saw it differently. In that moment, we had two choices - to look at the situation through the eyes of love or through the eyes of fear.

To look at the situation through the eyes of fear, would keep the intense feelings of negativity, sadness, uncertainty and stress magnified. Although these feelings were real and justified, they were never going to improve or change what was happening.

To look instead at the situation through the eyes of love, opened our minds to see what learning, what growth and what changes we could all collectively make on the back of this, to improve our lives and the way of the world. It united everyone – young and old – all over the world, in connecting and supporting one another. It demonstrated the human spirit of resilience. Being the light at that time and showing people another perspective, another way of thinking was so incredibly important.

You're not always going to feel bright and bubbly about life and that's okay. Whilst I encourage you to feel into your emotions, I also encourage you to start to see if there's another way. A different perspective, a lesson to be learnt, something bright that can come out of the dark. It's in those moments where we choose to be the light that we step up and inspire others to do the same. That is when the magic truly begins.

❋ ❋ ❋

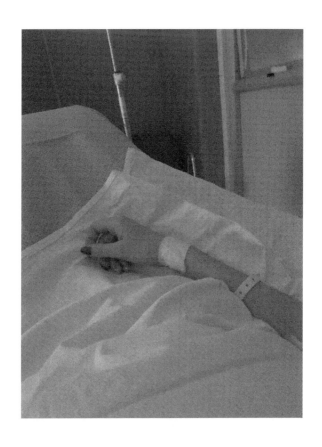

24. FEEL YOUR EMOTIONS

F eeling into your emotions is one of the healthiest ways we can be with ourselves. It might not seem like it at the time if you are having trouble breathing through your tears, but the alternative is far more destructive.

I've met some of the sweetest souls who seem on the surface to be quiet and calm but within them swirl a storm of emotions, which they go to great lengths to suppress. Often this suppression ends up manifesting itself in the form of anger, controlling behaviour or some other act of self-sabotage – none of which is healthy.

But why hide how you feel? Who is really benefiting from that? Not you – that's for sure.

Society has taken many steps forward in encouraging people to be more open about their feelings but sadly not everywhere is so progressive.

When I had my hospital moment in Palermo, Italy – I remember feeling like an absolute freak. I couldn't understand what the doctors were saying but the exasperated shaking of their hands in typical Italian style, indicated to me that they were puzzled as to why on earth I would want to harm myself and lose my zest for life. Of course, they were right in one respect, but on the other in that moment it created a wave of intense shame within me – not support.

I remember having to go for an interview in a Psychiatric ward with a formidable entrance door that was locked and alarmed. I remember being greeted on the other side by patients that with the greatest of respect, scared the hell out of me. Standing there in the pyjamas of my Earth Angel's Mumma, which were miles too short, fighting back the tears, trying in vain to get the doctor to understand in English that I had just reached a low moment and that I wasn't crazy – was something I will never, ever forget. In that moment I felt I lost my dignity, I felt isolated and I felt like I just didn't know who I was anymore. Thank God they saw within me that I didn't belong there – and I could return to my normal ward to recover.

I think it says a lot that the empowering people I follow on Instagram and YouTube helped me out of the fog of my emotions more than anyone professionally did. Clearly in different cultures, there is a lot of progression that still needs to be made in supporting those who struggle with their feelings.

I'm still a big believer though that feeling into your emotions is one of the most important things you can do. It's one thing though to cry, to allow your anger to bubble up or to feel the intensity of loneliness – it's quite another to do the work to support yourself through this, so that you can become a stronger, more empowered version of yourself.

Find the tools and techniques that will help you. For me Tapping has been an absolute game changer and has helped me to shift stagnant energies that were keeping me chained sub-consciously, to patterns of behaviour that no longer served me.

Asking for help, speaking with a counsellor or therapist, meditation, exercise, changing your environment, decluttering negative people, adopting daily habits that better support your highest self, cutting out alcohol, eating healthier – all are different techniques that can help. It's about discovering what works best for you.

The most important thing to remember is that you are never, ever alone. Reach out, find the strength inside even if it's as tiny as a grain of rice, do the work and recognise that you are on a journey. Don't beat up on yourself and don't compare your life to others.

Feeling into your emotions and then feeling through them with tools and techniques mean that you can come out the other side – and let your light shine.

"Your heart knows the way, run in that direction."

RUMI

25. LISTEN INWARDS

Our gut reaction. Our intuition. That teeny tiny voice inside that tells us to do one thing instead of another or tells us that things aren't quite what they seem. This is something we should totally pay more attention to.

Abraham Hicks references that inner knowing as being our Inner Being. They say that when we are feeling bad about a situation, it is because our Inner Being is thinking differently about it. Our Inner Being always knows what is best for us, even if at the time we cannot see it for ourselves.

This is why taking the time to be still, to breathe and to reflect is so important in learning to listen within. There are so many outside distractions that can influence us that often we ignore how we really feel about something, deep down. You see our feelings are where it all begins. They are our indicators as to where our focus is and on what ultimately, we are manifesting into our lives. Ignore them at your peril.

Meditation is one technique you can adopt to learn to connect with yourself more and to quieten your mind, so that you can be more open to inspired thoughts – which I consider to be like guidance from the Universe.

I first really understood the concept of inspired thoughts when I was manifesting my new life in Italy. I had written my Script about what I desired but I did not have a clue where to go from there – it was very much like I had just written a fairy-tale. Being still with myself though, I started to get ideas.

I got an idea of looking for Expat groups for people living in Italy, on Facebook. So, I joined some. Through these I found out about a voluntary skill-swap website called Workawayer – where people post from all around the world, skills that they need. In return you get free accommodation or something similar, for your time. Seeing that it covered Italy, I thought this could provide a fabulous opportunity to get to know what living in another country was really like, beyond a two-week holiday.

There was a subscription fee to pay to join for a year, which I didn't have the money right then to pay for. From deep within, I had the inspired thought to check the balance on a currency card which I had last used when I had been on holiday in Italy. The balance on the currency card covered the subscription fee in its entirety, with a couple of cents left to spare. So, I joined.

It was from this website that I made my connection

with a fabulous woman in Salerno, Italy, stayed with her and her family for four weeks teaching English and where I started to build the foundations for my life here. If I hadn't listened within to those inspired thoughts and connected with my feelings – what I wrote about in my Script may very well have stayed just a dream. This is why listening inwards is so powerful.

If the way you feel deep down is at conflict with how you think you want to feel about a situation, take the time to really listen to yourself. Often it is our ego that gets in the way – the part of us that wants to be right and in control about a situation.

Take a romantic rejection, for example. If you have been romantically rejected, there will be a part of your ego – even at a sub-conscious level – that wants to be in a position of power again, that wants to be proven right. With this in mind, your brain might be saying how you should get your ex back to prove a point when deep down your Inner Being is saying that the separation is actually for the best. Cue the conflict you feel.

At times like this though, it is about connecting with the feelings you have within – that's your guiding light – even if it feels painful to do so. This is where techniques such as Tapping help. Tapping is super effective at helping with clearing through the need to be right and the attachment we have to others.

When we make a commitment to ourselves to listen deep within, things start to shift. We begin to trust in ourselves more, in the way life plays out and in the experiences we have. We start to understand that within us is a pool of guidance that can help us to navigate life. We place less attention on the opinions of others and more on how we deep down feel about things. We ultimately begin to step up and into our infinite power.

* * *

26. STOP GIVING AWAY YOUR POWER

You've got to stop letting people into your lives who just take, take, take leaving you disempowered and depleted. Stop giving away your power. I say that to me as much as I say it to you.

There are many ways we give away our power in life – either consciously or sub-consciously. From letting our partner handle the finances, to passively letting others make all the decisions. From shying away from saying 'No' to lapping up breadcrumbs, like they're gold dust. From relying heavily on other people to always needing external validation.

When we give our power away, we are effectively saying we do not matter. **Except we do matter.**

So how can you take your power back? Here are some suggestions;

❉ ❉ ❉

Step up

If you give your power away by relying heavily on others – then it's time to learn to stand tall by yourself. Start living a more independent life, in whatever form that takes. Take control of your own finances, career prospects, friendships, living situation – whatever it may be. And if you are not sure how to do something – there is always Google. Google has the answer for everything.

* * *

Become comfortable with saying 'No'

This single word trips so many of us up. We get guilt complexes and we feel like we have to explain our lives away when we use it. But 'No' is a complete sentence all by itself. It doesn't require a 3000 word explanation, to back it up.

This word is a saving grace from situations we do not want to be a part of, to hanging out with people we know are not right for us to see. From being treated in a way which we know we don't deserve to filtering out life choices which we know do not serve us. It might feel difficult at first to be comfortable with saying 'No', but over time you will start to see how much more empowered you feel when you do.

* * *

Remember your Worth

Stop accepting breadcrumbs like they are some precious jewel. Remember that you deserve the best in all aspects of your life. This means that you remove yourself from people and situations that do not value you. It is as simple as that.

* * *

Self-Service

Stop waiting for other people to tell you that you are beautiful before you believe it. Stop waiting for other people to tell you that you should go for the promotion before you do. Stop waiting for other people to validate you.

Imagine if you were dependant on your partner to make you feel good. What if they had a bad day and weren't in the mood to tell you how incredible you were today? Would that mean that you would feel bad about yourself? Or, what if they weren't so excited about a business idea you had? Would that mean that you would start to have doubts? I mean come on. We give away our power in bucketloads when we wait on others to validate us. It's all about self-service; validate yourself first.

* * *

Make it a priority to look for the leaks in your life where your power slips away. Once you've identified them – then plug those gaps, step up and take your power back.

❃ ❃ ❃

27. IT'S NOT YOUR BUSINESS WHAT OTHERS THINK OF YOU

As true as this is, we often struggle with this concept. Like it or not as a society we sub-consciously feed of the validation from others. We allow ourselves to be influenced by the number of likes we get on our social media posts, by the opinions of friends and family and by the consensus of what is deemed socially acceptable. The truth is we cannot control the opinions and thoughts of others – so why let that bind you and stop you from living your life, the way you desire?

My decision to move to Italy wasn't one that everybody agreed with. I'm certain that people thought I was having some sort of a mid-life crisis at age 34 –

when in reality, it was an inner desire and calling that I just knew that I had to fulfil. If I hadn't been so in alignment with this – I could easily have started second-guessing myself and maybe even abandoning the idea completely.

This is why it is so important to start caring less what others think of us. Now I'm not saying this is an easy thing to do. It takes a degree of strength to be immune to how other people treat you or the things they say. Once you start tuning in to your inner self though about the choices you make – you will gradually start to care less and less.

Life is for living – in all its glorious technicolour detail – and when you are living your life this way and playing full out for your dreams, it's like an illuminous magnet for people's opinions. And often they aren't so positive. Why? Because when you are living a true, authentic life this triggers people. It reminds them of the dreams they haven't followed or the life they could have led, if they had made different choices. It shines the light on their blocks and shows the work they need to do within. This makes them feel uncomfortable and so their response is to throw some shade on you and what you're doing, to deflect it from themselves.

Now imagine if you allowed yourself to be swayed by others, knowing this. You would end up just the same as them and that would be an absolute shame.

Stop placing your attention on other people's opinions of you or what they might be saying – it's not going to make a blind bit of difference either way and is a whole heap of wasted energy. You will discover an incredible sense of freedom when you unchain yourself from the thoughts of others.

Stay connected and true to you. The right people will come into your life and become your cheerleaders but ultimately the biggest cheerleader you have is the one within yourself.

28. FILL YOUR OWN CUP FIRST

I t's an important part of life to be there for others. What's most important though is that you are there for yourself first. There's a reason why airlines tell you to put your own oxygen mask on first, before helping others with theirs.

Filling your own cup first is recognising that to truly be able to be of service to others, to give to others and to be there for them – it's vital that you feel good within yourself first and foremost. It's vital that you have nourished yourself with love, self-care and self-worth. It's vital that you are in the strongest position possible.

Fulfilling your own needs first is often viewed as a selfish act but I have a different take on it. I think that to give to others when you are already depleted yourself, *is* the selfish act. From that place you are not helping yourself and you certainly won't be as helpful to others as you think you will be. You'll have hidden resentments, you won't be coming at life from a high vibrational place and likely your energy will have a detrimental effect on those you wanted to help.

Fulfilling your own needs first is about learning to say 'No' to people and situations that aren't serving you, to events you aren't aligned with or to decisions you are not in agreement with. It's about having the confidence to want to feel good first and to do the work necessary to get you there. It's about knowing that when you are in that space you will serve as the shining example to those around you. Only then will you effect positive change and truly be able to be of service to others.

29. THE MAGIC OF MINDSET

The quality of your mindset is the difference in life between living the life you desire and talking about it. The difference between wallowing in your problems and overcoming them. Between having a breakdown and having a breakthrough.

Establishing a strong, determined mindset makes you unstoppable.

There are many excuses and reasons in life that we can attribute to having a less than healthy mindset. Whilst these might be valid, it is your personal responsibility to want to make the changes necessary to your mindset, to improve your life.

Mindset to me is like a muscle. If we neglect to put the work into it, it becomes weakened and cannot support us in the way it was intended. If, however we work that muscle every day, it becomes strong and helps to carry us through.

Having a determined mindset is what has helped me

over the years to do things that other people just didn't think was possible. Starting a business from scratch with no experience and making it successful, moving to a brand-new country not knowing the language or anyone and creating a life for myself, learning to carry on even when life around me looked bleak.

On the flip side I have many examples of people I have known in my life who demonstrated to me a weakened mindset. People who stayed in situations and with people who had emotionally hurt them, people who gave up on their dreams and goals the first time they had a wobble, people who complained about a situation but took no action to change it.

So how can we turn this around? How can you really tap into the power of your mindset? What improvements can you make to ensure that your mindset is tip top and on point? Here are some suggestions:

✽ ✽ ✽

Start feeding your mind with more positive, empowering content.

I never watch the news and although I do keep my toe dipped in the water about world events, I don't passively absorb them like a sponge. Why? Because the media has such a bias towards negative, fear-based, sensationalist stories that subconsciously it can be very easy to find yourself being affected by that. I make the conscious decision instead to watch something uplifting on YouTube, to read a book that is full of wisdom or to hang out with people that elevate me. Being aware of what we sub-consciously consume in our minds can be very eye-opening.

* * *

Learn to let go of people and situations that no longer serve you.

Stop clinging on with a tight grip to what no longer lights you up. The temporary hurt you may feel in making this decision will pass. Everything is temporary. In making this decision though you free yourself up to a life that truly serves you – and one that is a trillion times healthier for your mindset.

* * *

Move your body.

I'm not one for the gym but I do understand the importance of moving your body in strengthening your mindset. On the lazier days I may occasionally have, I really notice a difference in my mood and on what I feel is possible for my life. In contrast when I've been on the go all day or I have had a beautiful, refreshing walk by the sea in the sun I feel unstoppable.

Movement doesn't just have to come from the gym – walking, dancing or having a run are all valid!

* * *

Set yourself some dreams and goals.

Having a passion for something is an incredible thing. Whether it's pursuing a musical talent or learning a brand-new language – the focus on doing something that lights you up, engages your mind. Having goals fills you with new possibilities – all fantastic for your mindset.

* * *

Create a toolbox of techniques that serve you.

Life may very well deliver a moment which threatens to send your mindset into a tailspin. Having a toolbox of techniques available that you can turn to in those moments, can help you to course correct fast. For me Tapping is in my box as well as having access to incredible podcasts, books and You-Tube videos that can help to pull me out of a funk. Maybe meditation is a technique that helps you, or going for a run, or journaling. Whatever it may be, build your box of go-to tools, so you have something to turn to when the going gets tough.

✳ ✳ ✳

Most importantly of all remember this. Everything in life can teach us something, can help us grow, can delight us, can strengthen us, can help us to be the best version of ourselves possible. But how much enrichment we can take from it is dependent on one thing – and that's the strength of your mindset.

✳ ✳ ✳

"What hurts you, blesses you.
Darkness is your candle."

RUMI

30. IT'S ALL IN HOW YOU PERCEIVE IT

With anything in life, it is all in the way you perceive it. When I started my single life here in Italy, there were so many moments where I bought into the notion that I was lonely. I would consume myself with thoughts of what everyone else was getting up to or feel like I was missing out on something major. Whenever I had days where I didn't want to leave my house, I told myself that I would never meet new people or build upon the connections I already had. Until one day I woke up to a new possibility. I realised that yes, this could indeed continue to be how my life played out or I could choose to see things differently.

I could choose to see this moment in my life as an opportunity to have new experiences and adventures again, to rediscover the excitement I felt when I first moved here, to spend time on my dreams and goals and on looking for ways I could connect with new people and spend time with those people I did already know here. I started to fill myself with a sense of reassurance. This quelled the anxiousness I had felt and renewed my inner courageousness.

It's like that glass full or glass empty challenge – every situation can be seen in one of two ways – for its negatives or for its positives. To empower yourself though, I challenge you to start to see the less favourable moments in your life in a more positive way.

As I was editing this book, the Coronavirus Pandemic struck Italy and all of a sudden through the uncertainty of lockdown – perception provided a way to survive. Everywhere I looked people were being sucked into the vacuum of fear – worried for their families, their finances and their futures. It was an extremely surreal and sad moment but even from that space, it was possible to see things a different way.

The pause that this Pandemic forced the world into, was a major reset for us all. Suddenly our environments started to change – less cars on the roads meant the air became fresher, less pollution and disruption from boats meant the waters became clearer and sea life returned. Animals started to freely roam around the deserted streets. It was like Mother Earth took a deep exhale.

It also reset us as humans too. It taught us lessons of gratitude – in appreciating our health, our homes and our loved ones. It taught us to be less wasteful, as with limited shops open, we became more resourceful with the things we already had. It taught us to live in the moment – as future plans became entangled in question marks.

It taught us how technology – often heavily criticized prior to this, for being such a distraction to life – could unite us all in these times. Whether through social media, video calls or online meetings – we were able to connect, reconnect, strengthen and even repair our relationships with others. It taught us that it didn't matter where we were in the world, what our age or gender or skin colour was, what our jobs were or the type of house we lived in – it united us all. It taught us that we are all one.

By looking at this situation from these different perspectives, beautiful lessons emerged which if you had been stuck in a fear loop, you may very well have missed.

Global Pandemic aside, here are some other common challenges we may face in our life and how by perceiving things differently, things can shift for you.

* * *

Maybe you are struggling with your finances. This is the perfect time to first and foremost show appreciation and gratitude for what you do have. When we show love even for the pennies and cents – that energy encourages more. Take an inventory of the beliefs you have around money – often these stem back to childhood and how we saw our family manage their finances. Once you have identified the beliefs that no longer serve you in this area, do some Tapping to release them and replace them with more empowering ones. Educate yourself on financial matters – read the books, look on the Internet – knowledge is power.

Once you have done the inner work, then the outside actions are met with a lot less resistance. Look at the things you are spending your money on – are there services where you could get a better deal, things you need to stop – such as memberships you just don't use, ways you could be more resourceful – such as making your own coffee in the morning?

Socialise more mindfully by making the most of free events happening in your city, holding bring and share dinners with your friends, taking walks in local beauty spots. Look for the innovative ways you could bring more money in – is there a side hustle you'd like to begin? Or maybe is there another better paying job you could secure? I know exactly what it feels like to be a slave to your bank balance and to feel bloody helpless. That does nothing for you though – choosing instead to see your money worries as a blessing towards making better financial decisions – liberates you into the financial freedom you desire.

✽ ✽ ✽

Maybe you are battling an illness. This is the wake-up call to really look inwards at the thoughts you have and old resentments you may be holding onto. It's often thought that negativity in the body manifests itself into illness. With this in mind look at how you can improve your mindset so you can become more mentally strong. Look also at the lifestyle choices you have made and whether they really do serve you or whether there are improvements that can instead happen. Take this time to show love to your body – for love is an incredibly powerful emotion. Choose to see this time of illness, as the pathway to a deeper sense of appreciation and understanding of life.

❋ ❋ ❋

Maybe you are rebuilding your life again after a relationship breakdown. Use this experience to now build the life of your dreams. Get clear on what you will and won't tolerate going forward, discover your passions, set goals, meet new people, push yourself out of your comfort zone and be open to new adventures. Do the healing work on yourself, to free yourself from behaviours that did not serve you. View your relationship breakdown as the catalyst for your emotional breakthrough.

* * *

The next time life throws you a curveball, breathe, then take a moment to see if you can indeed look at things a different way.

* * *

"The wound is the place where the Light enters you."

RUMI

31. THE UNIVERSE ALWAYS HAS YOUR BACK

E ven when things are tough – I promise you this is so true. When you are able to step back and gain some perspective on your situation, there is always some growth, a lesson learnt or a new way of living that you may never have experienced had you not been through that.

We are always being guided – signs and synchronicities help to show us this – but ultimately it is whether we are open to them that makes all the difference.

We can choose to look at life through the lens of love or through the lens of fear. Every moment can be broken down into one of those two camps.

Looking at life through the lens of fear is commonplace in society, except that this is the very thing that keeps us stuck. It keeps us in the rut of repetitively making the same disempowering decisions and keeps us feeling despondent. We can easily tumble down the rabbit hole with this into a place of isolation and loneliness, a place where we have no direction, a place where life just doesn't feel good anymore. We disconnect ourselves from the Universe's guidance.

When we look at life through the lens of love we connect with our Inner Being. We look for the opportunities contained in the moment, the growth we can make, how we can improve on things even more. We have more compassion, empathy and a greater awareness of our worth. We come to understand that the Universe is working for us and not against us. We start to shift to a more positive way of thinking which in turn reflects back to us through our life experiences. We appreciate the present moment even more.

From this place of love, we start to recognise that everything around us is our teacher. From our work colleagues to our friends, from our family to our love relationships, from people that we really cannot stand to those we are secretly envious of. The Universe brings these people into our lives so that we can learn more about ourselves and have personal transformations that may otherwise have never come about.

There are many moments I can reflect back on in my life where I see evidence of this. From relationships that ended which hurt but when they did, I bloomed, to decisions I took in my life which others perhaps did not understand but proved to be the best thing that I could ever have done. From health scares which gave me a greater appreciation for my life to moments of feeling under the rocks which enabled me to discover my inner strength and follow my dream to help others.

When you really come to understand this concept, it creates a sense of freedom and reassurance. It focuses your attention away from the nitty grittiness of the moment to looking for the goodness contained within it and that shift in thinking will change your life.

32. BOUNDARIES ARE NON-NEGOTIABLE

Boundaries. You either have them or you don't. There's no middle ground.

If your boss keeps heaping work on you when you're already busy enough but instead of speaking up, you just become resentful - *you don't have boundaries*.

＊ ＊ ＊

If your friends only contact you when they want something, which you willingly help them with, but then they go AWOL for months – *you don't have boundaries*.

＊ ＊ ＊

If your lover isn't treating you right, but instead of talking about it with them, you can only tell your friends – *you don't have boundaries*.

✽ ✽ ✽

Boundaries look like this.

You communicate your needs clearly.

You ask for what you want.

You are prepared to step back from a situation, if it no longer serves you.

You prioritise your wellbeing and your feelings before everything else. (If you think this is selfish let me stop you right there – you simply cannot show up for others, if you don't show up for yourself first.)

You act out of willingness not obligation.

Boundaries are fluid in that they will mean different things to different people but essentially, it's all one of the same. Having boundaries is all about protecting you. It's about protecting your emotional wellbeing, your relationships, your joy. It's about being clear with people and teaching others just how to treat you.

When we stand strong and we communicate clearly to those around us what we will and won't tolerate in life, one of two things happens. People around us are either empowered to step up and deliver or they shrink and fall away – if that's the case, at least you know where you stand.

Life is simply too short to wake up everyday, filled with resentment, because you feel neglected or taken advantage of. Having boundaries results in a healthier, happier life.

It's not always easy to instil boundaries, especially if you are a recovering people pleaser like me. I know first-hand however, just how depleted you become when boundaries don't exist in your life.

When I ran my own business, I had zero boundaries. I would be working until super late every night doing admin, responding to emails, updating social media and working on the website. I often took on multiple bookings on the same day – which meant I had to travel across the UK, sometimes within a matter of hours – because I didn't want to disappoint or turn work away. My business became my life. I cancelled on friends and missed seeing my family. I was completely obsessed and close to burnout.

Life has shown me that it's blimming impossible to please everyone and you will only exhaust yourself in the process of trying. You need to value yourself enough to desire the healthiest of connections with others, the best treatment, the respect. If people don't want to give you that – then you need to ask yourself why they still have an all access pass to your life. Show them the exit door if they simply aren't willing to step up – regardless of who they are. Easier said than done maybe but trust me the alternative is far more damaging.

Boundaries aren't just what we put into place with our interactions with others. We can also create boundaries for ourselves. The way we treat ourselves and our bodies, the content we consume, how we spend our days, how we protect our dreams and goals, how long we spend on social media, the work we are willing to do on self-improvement and the list goes on.

Paradoxically having boundaries also creates a sense of freedom. These boundaries free us from the unhealthy expectations of others, from behaviour that does not serve us and from situations we don't feel aligned with.

Make setting boundaries your new non-negotiable. Start small if it scares you. Here are some general suggestions to help;

❋ ❋ ❋

Switch your phone to 'Do not Disturb' mode when you sleep – if people want to reach out to you, there's daytime! If there's an emergency, numerous calls will cancel out this mode – so you don't need to worry.

❋ ❋ ❋

If something isn't making you happy in your life, write it down. Writing helps with gaining a sense of clarity. From there you can choose to speak about your situation with those that can make a difference – the person or people concerned.

*　*　*

Set aside a designated amount of time per day to work on your dreams and goals. Even 30 minutes every day adds up.

*　*　*

Learn to say 'No' to situations that don't make you feel good, to spending time with people that don't elevate you or to things that you just do not want to do. This one small word is a powerful boundary all by itself.

*　*　*

Setting boundaries takes a bit of getting used to but when you do it will powerfully change your life, for the better.

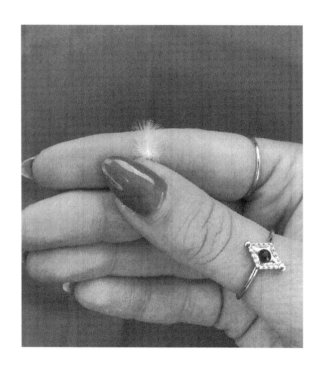

33. SIGNS & SYNCHRONICITIES

I have always regarded feathers as being a symbol of a loved one or Angel. They say that when a feather appears – an Angel is near.

The night before my Grandad died, a single white feather appeared on the floor of my room. I didn't know where it came from – until the next day I learnt of his passing – and then I understood.

I had been thinking of getting another tattoo and when this happened, I knew I wanted it to be of a feather. I wanted the tattoo on my hand but on the day, as I was walking to the tattoo shop, I started to get second thoughts. As I looked down on the ground, there lay a large feather right by my feet. I was certain then for my decision and it's one of the most beautiful tattoos I have.

A feather for me has become my sign and whenever I have moments of doubt, I usually always spot a feather that guides me and reminds me that it's all okay. Even today, as I was walking home, lost in my thoughts – a feather hopped, skipped and jumped in the wind along my path. It is truly beautiful.

How do you establish what can be a sign for you? It could be something that keeps presenting itself in your life – like feathers for me – or it could be something you feel a real connection towards or liking to. It is what feels good to you. Be open to your sign in your every-day life, especially when you are in need of guidance.

It's not just signs though that are incredibly powerful but also the way in which life plays out. I personally don't believe in coincidences – to me that implies that something happened outside of our control, it takes our power away. I believe in synchronicities – the moments of our life that harmonise and which lead us to what it is we are ultimately manifesting.

I have so many examples of synchronicities in my own life;

* * *

From deciding that I wanted to become an Entrepreneur to then learning of a business that was up for sale. To essentially just ending up buying boxes of china and a Facebook page to then rebranding, building a business and turning it into a six-figure reality.

* * *

From writing a Script of wanting to create a new life for myself in Italy to how every single event unfolded to then make that my life.

* * *

From starting to get into the Law of Attraction and manifesting in 2014 to then realising that I had been gifted *'The Secret'* – the famous Law of Attraction book, a few months prior, and had forgotten all about it.

* * *

It really is about being open to the magic of life. When you set intentions, you trust in the process, you surrender – which basically means you stop asking over and over again for what you want, because it just cannot come to you if you don't give it a chance and you listen inwards to the inspired thoughts you have – synchronicities will present themselves in ways you never thought possible.

* * *

34. BE YOUR OWN CHEERLEADER

As I'm writing this, I'm sitting by the sea in a part of Salerno, Italy, affectionately known as 'Salifornia'- the palm trees make people think of California, so they blended the two names! The sun is beautifully warm, the sky is an array of blues and the distant music playing from the beach hut bar, fills the air. I have to pinch myself into remembering it is still February.

Today is a significant day because it is exactly two years ago since I first ever came to Salerno. I came to teach English, in a cultural exchange – to an incredible woman and stayed with her family – who in turn showed me around and taught me about Italian culture. That experience changed my life and I am so happy to have the amazing friendships and connections today, that that brought about.

Back then my life here was a dream – I knew nobody

other than these people, I did not speak the language, I didn't have a job, a home – anything. Now two years later, I have made that dream come true. In fact, I made it come true in just 6 months. I really am a phenomenal woman.

Today reminded me of how in life, it's all about being your own biggest cheerleader. It's nobody else's responsibility to tell you how incredible, inspirational and superb you are. Other people may not want to praise you for their own blocks and limiting behaviours. If you have people in your life who do, then cherish them, they're the best people in the world! For the most part though, it's your job alone to praise yourself and celebrate what you achieve in life. And that you must.

Writing this book for me has been all about wanting you to remember your worth and empowering you to be the best version of yourself possible, at a time when I was learning that for myself too. Celebrating your achievements and just how far you've come, is just one way that you can do this.

Take the time, even if it's just once a week or month, to reflect on what you have achieved over that period. As far as I'm concerned there's nothing too small to celebrate – from not texting an ex who didn't appreciate your worth right through to any incredible career moves you've made or money that's come your way. It all deserves a pat on the back.

When we make a conscious decision to look for the

good in our lives we become like a magnet for uplifting experiences and things that we can praise ourselves for. It's all about your point of focus. Energy flows where your attention goes.

Don't wait on anyone to tell you how amazing you are. Go tell yourself that. Every single day.

* * *

35. TAKE YOURSELF OUT OF YOUR HEAD

I'm certain that you have experienced what I call a mind movie. Those moments when you get lost in your own head, in your own thoughts and create a movie for yourself of how you think a situation will play out or why things happened a certain way. Often there is nothing founded in what you are thinking – it's just the meaning that you have placed on a moment.

I have been guilty of this a lot. When I have experienced a relationship breakdown my thoughts will go into overdrive, with all the perceived reasons why it happened and what I think my ex is now getting up to. The thing is a lot of these thoughts are complete and utter bullshit – my mind movie is being solely directed by my insecurities.

You can create mind movies about almost anything in your life. Perhaps a friend takes a couple of days to reply to your message – your mind movie starts playing that you have done something to upset them. Perhaps you didn't get the promotion at work – your mind movie starts playing that you just aren't worthy of it. Perhaps you don't have many friends and everyone around you does – your mind movie starts playing that there is something wrong with you and that you will never be popular. Perhaps it seems like you never have enough money – your mind movie starts playing that you don't deserve financial success and that you wouldn't be able to handle it, if you did.

It is time to do another take. It is time to take yourself out of your head.

Our mind movies are as a result of insecurities and doubts we are sub-consciously holding onto, so the first place to start is to clear those out. Tapping is my go-to technique for this – I really find that it shifts the energies within me. Some issues can take a few rounds of tapping to release – especially if my grip has been tight on them – whilst others can be released after just one Tapping session. I highly recommend trying it.

If Tapping isn't for you – find something that is – journaling is another way of releasing from us and seeing in black and white just what our insecurities are. Sometimes the realisation of this alone, can be enough for you to want to take steps to change things.

It is all about empowering ourselves more and creating a different movie. It is about creating a movie of possibility and of what it is you desire. It is about releasing the attachment you may have towards what other people think about you. It is all about recognising that you are the creator of your life story.

Taking yourself out of your head is about freeing yourself from the constraints that your limiting behaviours place you in and of taking the big step into your innate power.

❋ ❋ ❋

36. TIME TO BLOOM

It's taken me some time but now I truly understand the concept that life happens for you and not to you. Everything - the good, the bad, the shame, the shit, the joy, the elation - it is all shaping you to be the best version of yourself possible. When you move yourself from a place of 'poor me' and pity, you can really begin to see this for yourself.

To bloom in life, means that you take all of the lessons these various moments have taught you and you turn them into something spectacular - however that looks for you.

As I write these last few words of my book, it's been six months since I was in that hospital bed in Palermo, Italy, unsure for myself and for my life. Back then, this book was just a thought in my mind and now here it is, in your hand with a message of support to share to the world.

I want you to remember one thing - in life you can absolutely overcome anything. The most devasting hardships, the suffocating feelings of loss and bereavement, the pain of abuse, the betrayals, the judgements, the loneliness, the heartache, the unworthiness, the guilt, the sadness, the financial set-backs - I know because I have done just that.

Writing this book has been my very own blooming moment - the culmination of the lessons I have learnt and the strength I have gained to be the woman I am today.

Like a flower in the wild thrives in the rain - use your uncomfortable moments to grow.

It is time now for you to bloom.

BONUS CHAPTERS

EMPOWERING INSTAGRAM ACCOUNTS

Social Media can provide inspiring and uplifting content – if you know where to look. These are the standout accounts I follow and absolutely love for their empowering messages and pearls of wisdom, that have helped me in my lowest moments. I hope you gain something nutritious from them too.

@GalaDarling

@NataliaBenson

@GabriellaRosie

@Vexking

@theslumflower

@cleowade

@msrachelhollis

@marieforleo

@yesandyourlife

@aaronxrose

@melrobbins

@jayshetty

@oprah

@jerico.mandybur

@sarablakely

@gabbybernstein

@morganharpernichols

@queercosmos

@artbysarahanne

@fionabarkerdesign

@sophiaamoruso

@gabbybernstein

@tinybuddhaofficial

It's one thing to passively follow an account, it's quite

another to follow through on the words that resonate with you and allow them to change your life.

Let me know who you discover as a result of this list or share your own discoveries. Tag me @lovefromclaire on my Instagram and I'll share your wisdom.

BOOKS TO LIGHT YOU UP

R eading for me is like nourishment for the soul. I literally devour books and the lessons contained within them.

These are the books that made a profound difference in my life and continue to do so even now. Because the best books are the ones you want to revisit again and again.

"If one cannot enjoy reading a book over and over again, there is no use in reading it at all." – Oscar Wilde

Ask and it is Given -Esther & Gerry Hicks

The Big Leap – Gay Hendricks

The Universe Has Your Back – Gabrielle Bernstein

The Wisdom of Sundays – Oprah Winfrey

Radical Self Love – Gala Darling

The Secret – Rhonda Bryne

The Alchemist – Paulo Coehlo

Good Vibes, Good Life – Vex King

Heart Talk – Cleo Wade

Game Changers – Dave Asprey

You are a Badass at Making Money – Jen Sincero

Think and Grow Rich – Napoleon Hill

Lucky Bitch - Denise Duffield-Thomas

Get Rich, Lucky Bitch - Denise Duffield-Thomas

Abundance Now – Lisa Nicholls

The 5 Second Rule – Mel Robbins

Girl, Stop Apologizing – Rachel Hollis

What A Time To Be Alone – Chidera Eggerue

Everything is Figureoutable – Marie Forleo

Super Attractor – Gabrielle Bernstein

She Means Business – Carrie Green

Daily Oracle – Jerico Mandybur

Miracles Now - Gabrielle Bernstein

How To Get Over A Boy - Chidera Eggerue

Chillpreneur - Denise Duffield-Thomas

Eat, Pray, Love - Elizabeth Gilbert

You'll See It When You Believe It - Wayne Dyer

The Four Agreements - Don Miguel Ruiz

E-Squared - Pam Grout

Let me know who you end up adding to your reading list or another incredible book you've read – I love discovering new titles! Tag me @lovefromclaire on Instagram and I'll share your wisdom.

❋ ❋ ❋

YOUTUBE CHANNELS TO FOLLOW

I often treat YouTube like an Oracle. When a channel is suggested to me based on what YouTube thinks I'll like, I follow through. Nearly always there is something on that channel that speaks to me or is exactly what I'm going through at that moment in my life. The Universe is always guiding us.

Below are the channels I follow and love, some I found myself, others I was guided to but all of them are empowering, thought provoking and brilliant.

Lewis Howes – School of Greatness

Gala Darling

Lumiere Tarot

Mel Robbins

Lisa Nicholls

Dating Guy

The Gem Goddess

Roxy Talks

Master Sri Akarshana

Create Your Future

Abraham Hicks

Brad Yates

Let me know what channels you add based on this list and also which are your favourites. Tag me @lovefrom-claire on Instagram and I'll share your wisdom.

✻ ✻ ✻

"I found myself."

RUMI

ACKNOWLEDGEMENTS

A heartfelt thank you to Sarah Watt for the beautiful cover art and illustrations throughout my book. Follow your dreams - you have a real gift.

About Sarah Watt

Sarah Watt has always had a talent for art and design. After putting her passion aside to pursue careers in the banking industry and later the emergency services, as well as raise a family, Sarah is now once again pursuing her passion for her artwork. Her recent experience with endometriosis has given her much needed time to reflect and explore her creative side once more.

Instagram - @artbysarahanne

ABOUT THE AUTHOR

Claire Hearn

 Claire Hearn is a former Police Officer and multi-award winning Entrepreneur. She has previously won awards from business magnate Theo Paphitis, Jacqueline Gold CBE and her business was named one of the U.K's Top 100 Small Businesses, where she enjoyed a private reception at 10 Downing Street.

Having changed her life over and relocated to Italy, she became passionate about wanting to share the life experiences and lessons she had learnt along the way, to inspire and empower others.

Claire always loved writing from a young age and having been told she had the writer's fork on her palm when she was a teenager, she decided to follow her passion. 'Wake Up to Your Worth' is her first book.

When Claire isn't writing, she enjoys photography, being by the sea in the sun and sipping an Aperol Spritz with a splash of vodka.

Printed in Great Britain
by Amazon